# Blessed Beyond Measure

## DEVOTIONAL JOURNAL

# Blessed

## BEYOND MEASURE

### DEVOTIONAL JOURNAL

## Gloria Copeland

NEW YORK   BOSTON   NASHVILLE

Unless otherwise noted, Scriptures are taken from the King James Version of the Bible.

Scriptures noted AMP are taken from the Amplified® Bible. Copyright © 1954, 1962, 1965, 1987 by The Lockman Foundation. Used by permission.

Scriptures noted NIV are taken from the HOLY BIBLE: NEW INTERNATIONAL VERSION®. Copyright © 1973, 1978, 1984 by International Bible Society. Used by permission of Zondervan Publishing House. All rights reserved.

Scriptures noted NKJV are taken from the NEW KING JAMES VERSION. Copyright © 1979, 1980, 1982, Thomas Nelson, Inc., Publishers.

Scriptures noted NLT are taken from the *Holy Bible*, New Living Translation, Copyright © 1996, 2004. Used by permission of Tyndale House Publishers, Inc., Carol Stream, Illinois 60188. All rights reserved.

Scriptures noted NASB are taken from the NEW AMERICAN STANDARD BIBLE®, Copyright © 1960, 1962, 1963, 1968, 1971, 1972, 1973, 1975, 1977, 1995 by The Lockman Foundation. Used by permission.

Scriptures noted TLB are taken from *The Living Bible*, copyright © 1971. Used by permission of Tyndale House Publishers, Inc., Wheaton, Illinois 60189. All rights reserved.

FaithWords
Hachette Book Group
237 Park Avenue
New York, NY 10017

www.faithwords.com

Book design by Fearn Cutler de Vicq
Printed in the United States of America

First Edition: October 2010
10 9 8 7 6 5 4 3 2 1

FaithWords is a division of Hachette Book Group, Inc.
The FaithWords name and logo are trademarks of Hachette Book Group, Inc.

Library of Congress Cataloging-in-Publication Data

Copeland, Gloria.
    Blessed beyond measure devotional journal / Gloria Copeland.—1st ed.
       p. cm.
    ISBN 978-0-446-53907-4
    1. God (Christianity)—Goodness—Prayers and devotions.   I. Title.
    BT137.C67 2010
    231'.5—dc22

                                                        2010006173

# CONTENTS

# INTRODUCTION

*A* few years ago, the Spirit of the Lord spoke to my heart very clearly. He said, *Preach the goodness of God and fear not the reproach of men.*

*The goodness of God.*

It sounded like a simple subject at the time. But as I began to search out what the Bible has to say about God's goodness, I found it was a theme that ran from Genesis to Revelation. The more I studied about it, the more I found. It absolutely amazed me to see how much the Scriptures talked about the goodness of God. My book, *Blessed Beyond Measure*, was the result of my studies.

Since that time, the message of that book has remained close to my heart. I have come to realize that many people have an incorrect concept of God, which hinders them from coming to Him and receiving what Jesus' death and resurrection purchased for them. At one time, I was one of those people. I'm so glad I found out the truth! Now I want everyone else to know it, too. You see, God loves every person and He wants to do them good.

The Bible pretty well sums it up when it says, "For God so loved the world, that he gave his only begotten Son." The Bible also says, "God is love" (1 John 4:8). Because of this great love, each person who is willing can receive salvation, healing, deliverance, peace, blessings, and every other good thing God promised us in His Word. In fact, understanding and believing the goodness of God is the very foundation for our faith. This may not sound at all like what you have heard about God all your life, but it is the truth. The Bible says truth is what will make you free.

In this devotional journal, based on my book *Blessed Beyond Measure*, you are about to discover the freeing truth about the nature of God and how much He wants to bless you. In fact, every page speaks of His goodness so that this foundational truth can be written on your heart by the time you are finished.

This devotional journal offers nine sections that parallel a chapter in the original book. Each section features five days' worth of material with four daily elements to encourage you: a short devotional reading, a reflection question, a personal application question, and a page for writing out your prayers. The reflection question, called "Reflecting on His Goodness," explores the main theme of the day while the application question, called "Experiencing His Goodness," will help you integrate what you've read into your day-to-day life, making it even more personal. And throughout each day of material, you'll find verses from Scripture to lift your heart.

The act of writing can increase and multiply what God is revealing, so there's room throughout this book for you to not only record the answer to each question but to write out your prayers. Treat each day's concluding journal page, "Praying in His Goodness," as an opportunity. An opportunity to bring your intimate prayers and thoughts before the throne of grace in a fresh way—written in your own hand. You'll be amazed at what God will do through your daily interactions with Him.

As you consider and experience God's goodness throughout this book, expect Him to open up His storehouse of blessings to you. He has already made plans and provisions to do just that.

How can this good news become reality in your life? You need only open up your heart and receive. Begin by praying the prayer for yourself that Paul prayed for the Ephesians in Ephesians 3:16–21:

Dear Heavenly Father, I pray that You would grant me, according to the riches of Your glory, that I be strengthened with might by Your Spirit in my inner man, that Christ—the Anointed One—may dwell in my heart by faith. That I, being rooted and grounded in love, may be able to comprehend, understand, and have in-depth, working knowledge with all the saints what is the breadth, and length, and depth, and height of the most powerful thing that exists. Let me know the very love of You Yourself—the love with which You love Jesus—which passes all human knowledge. Give me the knowledge of this love, Father, that I might be filled with all the fullness of God, because 1 Corinthians 13 says that love "never fails"! Now unto You, Father—who are able to do exceeding abundantly above all that I ask or think, according to the power that is working in all of me right now—unto You be glory in me, and in the church by Christ Jesus throughout all ages, world without end. Amen.

...Then read on, and remember: God is not mad at you. He loves you. He is a good God. Understanding this will change your life!

*Gloria Copeland*

# Blessed Beyond Measure

## DEVOTIONAL JOURNAL

*Understanding God's Goodness—The Foundation of Faith*

## Day One

## The Goodness of God

*[What, what would have become of me] had I not believed*
*that I would see the Lord's goodness in the land of the living!*
Psalm 27:13 AMP

Why do you suppose the Bible—from front to back, Old Testament and New—would so strongly emphasize the simple truth that God is good?

Because it is the foundation of our faith in Him.

The more we know God's goodness, the more we trust Him. The more we trust Him, the easier it is for us to put our lives into His hands. And only by placing our lives in His hands can we open the way for Him to save us, and bless us, and work through us, so that His wonderful will can be done on earth as it is done in heaven. God wants to bless you physically. He wants to bless you in your finances, in your relationships, and in your career. He wants to give you the desires of your heart.

My prayer is that as you read and use this journal, the revelation of God's goodness will help you receive from Him whatever you need.

## Reflecting on His Goodness

What is the connection between knowing that
God is good and trusting Him in your life?

I in having my first Women's retreat.
God presence is all around me. I believe
I in recieving His best. My counseling course
has allow my husband & I to reflection
on how God wants us to relate to each other
in a more intemiate & respectful, love & concern
way. Communication is the key. Knowing the
difference between manipulation & ministry.
Manipulation is selfish state of being focusing
on only fulfulling own needs. Security &
significance can only be found in God. We
can only naturally enchance the security
& significance. God is mindful of marriages
& by his Spirit they can overcome any
obstacles in there way.

*So don't be afraid, little flock. For it gives your Father great happiness*
*to give you the Kingdom.*

(Luke 12:32 NLT)

## Experiencing His Goodness

Have there been times in your life when you did not know
or believe that God is good? How were those times different from
your periods of unquestioning trust in God?

I wasn't feel good this morning, I started professing by His stripe I was healed. God healed all manner of sickness & disease. The took my confession & took healing me right on the spot. Thank you Jesus. I trust God completely. I have nothing else to stand on. He's everything to me. This year a shift has taken place in my spirit I want to obey Him more. I want to grasp & hold everything He has for me. When I experience God goodness it mostly when He touches people thru me. Although this year I want the manifestation. Kim Clement (Prophet) say, God said "This was the year of the Woman" I believe him. I'm crying because the power of the Lord is upon. His goodness is penetrating my heart.

*Many are the sorrows of the wicked, but he who trusts in, relies on, and confidently leans on the Lord shall be compassed about with mercy and with loving-kindness.*

(Psalm 32:10 AMP)

## Praying in His Goodness

I have seen God goodness in my personality. My prayer is that God give me the patience & understanding of His people. I pray that His goodness show as an example through me His love towards others. I pray that God give me the strength to show His goodness to my husband & children. family members & co-worker.

I pray that allow me to see His goodness for my life. I pray that I will always appreciate & cherish it.

*Day Two*

## Trust Him with Your Life

*Be of good cheer! It is I; do not be afraid.*
Matthew 14:27 NKJV

Wouldn't you like to go further in your walk with God? Wouldn't you like to be more bold and daring in your faith?

Until you settle the fact that God is good and you can trust Him with your Life, your faith is never going to be great because you will always draw back in fear. You will always be thinking, *What if He doesn't come through for me? What if He is not listening to me? What if He asks me to do something that will harm me in some way?*

However, once your heart grasps the goodness of God, you won't be plagued by those questions. You'll be confident in the fact that He will never hurt you. He will never abandon you or let you down. As long as you follow Him, He will always be there—loving you, helping you, and blessing you.

If He asks you to, you'll be bold enough to walk on the water because you know His goodness will support you and keep you afloat.

## Reflecting on His Goodness

Think of times when you heard God say, "Come!" but you didn't step out of your comfort zone. What do you think stopped you?

Most of the time finances keeps me from moving out. I'm being challenge in that area now. I'm planning a women's retreat, I have to put a large desposit but don't have enough commit women to go yet. I'm senda check for 600.00 my faith. I believe God will do exceedly & abundantly all I can ask or think. This year is the year I will walk out on the water. Years pass fear would have grip me. I want what God has for me like never before. I have turn my back on the fears, tears, pass disappointment, people opinions. I want to be used by God. Bid me Lord, I trust you with all my heart & soul.

*So He said, "Come." And when Peter had come down out of the boat,*
*he walked on the water to go to Jesus.*

(Matthew 14:29 NKJV)

## Experiencing His Goodness

If you totally trusted God with your life today, how might it be different? What fears would you like to turn over to Him?

Fear of not having enough money or resource or support. He is truly all to me now.

*The LORD is on my side; I will not fear. What can man do to me?*
(Psalm 118:6 NKJV)

## Praying in His Goodness

Lord, I thank for this opportunity to
be used by you. God fill me with every
spiritual gift to succeed in what you have
call me to do. Lord, I pray for desire
correct & favor. I pray for boldness &
clarity of your voice. Thank You Lord for
teaching me how to move-out on
faith.

## Day Three

## Does God Bring Suffering?

*The LORD is gracious and full of compassion, slow to anger and great in mercy.*
*The LORD is good to all, and His tender mercies are over all His works.*
Psalm 145:8–9 NKJV

Traditional religion has made people think they couldn't depend on the goodness of God. Religion has taught that one day God might make you sick. The next day He might make you poor. Some have even said that God gives you things like sickness and poverty to bless you.

But that is contrary to the written Word of God. God is not confused about good and evil. He has figured out what's good for us and what's not. He knows it's good when we have more than enough natural provision in our lives. He knows it's good for our children to be blessed and for us to be physically healthy and whole.

On the other hand, He knows it's evil for us to be sick, poor, frightened, and oppressed. Actually, the Hebrew word *shalom* that the Lord uses so frequently to bless His people means to have wholeness in your life—spirit, soul, and body. It means you have nothing missing, nothing broken. God knows that is the way things ought to be, and that is the way He wants them to be—not just for a few of His people but for every one of them.

## Reflecting on His Goodness

Have you been told that God is the source of all things—good *and* bad—that happen to us? Do you believe that? As you reflect on it now, what is wrong with that kind of thinking?

I believe everything that God does is good. I believe our own personal sin causes evil to come upon our life. On another person action through sin harms another person life. I believe God teaches us how to defeat our sinful nature that His goodness maybe exhibit in our daily life. I believe if God wanted evil to fall upon us. there would of been no need for Jesus to die at calvary.

*The LORD shall preserve you from all evil; He shall preserve your soul.*

(Psalm 121:7 NKJV)

## Experiencing His Goodness

Read Psalm 23 in your favorite translation. Are you going through a "valley" today? Paraphrase a verse or the whole psalm that will help you find in this situation the same confidence and trust that David had.

*As I walk through life by the spirit ~~my~~ my safety & assurance will rest in the love I have for Jesus Christ. I do not fear what man will do or say to me.*

*Yes, though I walk through the [deep, sunless] valley of the shadow of death, I will fear or dread no evil, for You are with me; Your rod [to protect] and Your staff [to guide], they comfort me.*

(Psalm 23:4 AMP)

## Praying in His Goodness

I pray that my ears & eye gate are cover in the Blood of Jesus. I bind any false teaching or docrines to dwell or rest in my spirit. I pray a hedge of protection around my family & love one. The strangers voice we will not follow.

*Day Four*

## Remember His Goodness

*Praise the* LORD, *O my soul, and forget not all his benefits—who forgives all
your sins and heals all your diseases, who redeems your life from the pit and
crowns you with love and compassion, who satisfies your desires with good things
so that your youth is renewed like the eagle's.*

Psalm 103:2–5 NIV

When I think of someone in the Bible who truly understood the goodness
of God, one person that always comes to mind is David. David not only knew
about the goodness of God, he had seen it work in his life. He had seen the
victories God's goodness gained for him, and just thinking of them made him
bold.

You and I will be the same way. The more we understand the goodness of
God and the more we see that goodness operating in our lives, the more victories we will have to remember. The more victories we remember, the harder
it is for the devil to talk us into letting him run over us. When the devil tries
to convince us that he's going to defeat us this time, he won't be able to do it.
We'll remember victory over the lion and the bear in our own lives and think,
*You know, God got me this far. He will not let me down now!*

## Reflecting on His Goodness

Read 1 Samuel 17:34–37. What made David so bold when facing his giant, Goliath? What principle did he follow that would help us when we are facing our giants?

God has not given me the spirit of fear; but love, power & sound mind. My boldness comes from the heart of God. He has placed a desire to the captive free. I walk by His power & might without it none of what I do would be possible. I love going into the battle field for the Lord. Like right now I'm in a warfare within myself. I feel hurt, disappointed & abandonment but that does not deter me from moving forward. it makes have even more spiritual passion to win. God goodness will carry me through. When I'm weak He make me strong. Jesus that you for purpose, dynasty, & life. I love you Lord.

*The LORD that delivered me out of the paw of the lion, and out of the paw of the bear,*
*he will deliver me out of the hand of this Philistine.*

(1 Samuel 17:37)

## Experiencing His Goodness

On this page, recall (remember) the specific things God
has blessed you with in your life, reflecting His extraordinary
goodness toward you and your family.

God has given me a miracle daughter
name Naomi Testimony Smith. The doctor
say she had fluid on her brain, to abort her
8 times, she wouldn't walk, talk, or eat on
her own. She this talkative running, jumping
eating beautiful little girl. Nehemiah was
diagnosed with seizures however God has blessed
him not to have them frequent and recently
not at all. Thank Jesus for this us.
I thank you keeping us when we were
homeless, broke, hurt, and rob from
every spiritual joy.

*For You are my hope; O Lord God, You are my trust from my youth and
the source of my confidence. Upon You have I leaned and relied from birth;
You are He Who took me from my mother's womb and You have been my benefactor
from that day. My praise is continually of You.*

(Psalm 71:5–6 AMP)

## Praying in His Goodness

My prayer is that Shafii, Sharifa + Shaneka experience God goodness in their lives. I pray that they recognize Him as their ultimate source for all they deserve. I come against ever stronghold over their minds, body + soul. I plead the blood of Jesus to deliver them from self. I pray Shaneka open her heart to you. I pray a hedge of protection around her. I break every stronghold in her mind; lust, idolatry, sexual immorality, homosexuality, drunkenness. Jamal be cleanse from all unrighteousness. Touch them now Lord I pray.

*Day Five*

## Where Will You Be Next Year?

*Therefore put on every piece of God's armor, so you will be able to resist the enemy*
*in the time of evil. Then after the battle you will still be standing firm.*
Ephesians 6:13 NLT

If you're still somewhat skeptical, let me ask you a question. Where will you be this time next year if you don't start believing to see the goodness of the Lord in the land of the living? You'll be right where you are now. Things will be no better in your life. In fact, they'll probably be worse because the devil will still be unhindered in his work to steal, kill, and destroy.

But if you'll find out what the Bible says about God's goodness and you'll dare to believe it, things will begin to change in a wonderful way. Your life will immediately begin to improve. A year from now, you'll not only see that goodness on the pages of your Bible, you'll see it around you every day of your life.

That's what I call *living!*

## Reflecting on His Goodness

What did God do through Jesus that proves He wants to bless us
in every part of our lives?

God give Jesus healing power, deliverance, compassion, give Jesus all power, through resurrection God has show his goodness by providing me with the same resurrection power. I'm more than a conquer, God has given me the Holy Spirit to help + direct in my spiritual journey. If am willing + obedient God will manifest His glory in my life.

*He that spared not his own Son, but delivered him up for us all,*
*how shall he not with him also freely give us all things?*

(Romans 8:32)

## Experiencing His Goodness

What do you think your life will be like this time next year
if you don't start believing in the goodness of the Lord?
How would you describe where you are now and
where you would like to be next year?

1/27/2011

Right now there is a year of transition.
I believe God is setting me up with one
of the biggest blessings in my life.
I will see salvation of my daughter
Shareka, Marriage whole, Ministry flourish
Nehemiah do exceed abundantly all I
think or ask in his academics, Beautiful
Home, New Car. I want to give in
the Million for the Kingdom of God.
I believe prosperity is chase me down.
I believe God will paid my tuition
in full. My master program will guilded
strictly by the Holy Spirit.

1/29/2011
      Shareka dedicated her life to
Christ. My daughter has a new
beginnings.

*He lifted me out of the slimy pit, out of the mud and mire; he set my feet on a
rock and gave me a firm place to stand.*

(Psalm 40:2 NIV)

## Praying in His Goodness

My prayer is for the Jews survivors from the Holocaust. No weapon formed against Israel shall prosper. I pray Lord that I can become a wealth transference to your people & your goal upon they earth. God allow me to be your precious vessel. God, I just heard Pastor Benny Hinn testimony. Your favor is fabulous, fantastic, forever, fragrance.

Shaneka has given her life back to you Lord. God thank you for your goodness. Protect Shaneka & guard her. I pray her spiritually understand be awakening by your Holy Spirit. Holy Spirit guide her into all Spiritual Truth. Father I'm so bless that your answer your hand maiden prayer. Am truly grateful. I Thank you, Thank you. I love you Lord.

## Will the Real God Please Stand Up?

### Day One

# Images of God

*The Lord is gracious and full of compassion, slow to anger and abounding in mercy and loving-kindness. The Lord is good to all, and His tender mercies are over all His works.*
Psalm 145:8–9 AMP

Ever since the Garden of Eden the devil has been devising schemes to separate people from God. And the one scheme that seems to have worked the best for him is causing them to doubt God's goodness.

Even religions based on Christianity have portrayed God in ways that are totally contrary to the truths revealed by the Bible. Religious art, for example, often pictures everybody sad. Long-faced preachers have represented God as mad at the whole human race and looking furiously for someone to punish.

If you have been made wary of God by those kinds of religious traditions, it's important for you to know the Bible does not reveal a God who is out to "get us" or to do us harm in any way. The fact is the Bible does not portray God being in a bad mood; you never catch Him having a bad day. God is love every day. His mercy endures forever!

## Reflecting on His Goodness

Have you ever, like Eve, been convinced that God was trying to deprive you rather than protect you? Hold out on you rather than bless you? Where did that thinking come from?

2/19/2011 I heard from my brother after 6 six years. I'm so fill with so many emotion, what am sure of is God as truly blessed my soul. What a joy. Troy, big brother I love you)

*Every good gift and every perfect gift is from above, and comes down from the Father of lights, with whom there is no variation or shadow of turning.*

(James 1:17 NKJV)

## Experiencing His Goodness

Take one current situation in your life where you believe Satan is trying to influence your thinking. Write out a prayer that specifically asks for God's gracious intervention in dispelling the enemy's influence in this area of your life.

_I pray to you, O LORD, in the time of your favor; in your great love,_
_O God, answer me with your sure salvation._

(Psalm 69:13 NIV)

# Praying in His Goodness

## Day Two

## God's Favorite Pastime

*It was God [personally present] in Christ, reconciling and restoring the world
to favor with Himself, not counting up and holding against [men] their
trespasses [but cancelling them], and committing to us the message
of reconciliation (of the restoration to favor).*
2 Corinthians 5:19 AMP

It is not just Christian religious tradition that has depicted God as angry and vindictive. People who worshiped demon gods throughout history often believed they had to hurt themselves or someone they loved in order to appease their gods' anger. Other pagan gods were not so harsh, yet it seemed they all needed something, offerings of fruit or gifts of some kind, to make them happy.

But our God is not like that! We don't have to do penance or make sacrifices to appease Him. He Himself has already provided the sacrifice for sin in the person of His Son. The moment we receive Jesus as Savior and Lord, we find that God is already happy with us. What He's doing now is looking for opportunities to do us good and show us favor.

You know how people who have hobbies like fishing or golf are always looking for opportunities to do those things? You might say God's favorite pastime is doing good.

God wants to give good gifts to people. It's what He loves and enjoys. He is Jehovah the Good.

# Reflecting on His Goodness

In what ways have you tried to appease God?
How do people try to do that today?

_____

_____

_____

_____

_____

_____

_____

_____

_____

_____

_____

_____

_____

_____

_____

_____

_____

_____

*The LORD your God is with you.... He will take great delight in you, he will quiet*
*you with his love, he will rejoice over you with singing.*

(Zephaniah 3:17 NIV)

## Experiencing His Goodness

Who in your life enjoyed doing good for you? How has that made a difference in your view of God?

_____

_____

_____

_____

_____

_____

_____

_____

_____

_____

_____

_____

_____

_____

_____

_____

_____

_____

_____

_____

_____

_____

*If you then, being evil, know how to give good gifts to your children, how much more will your Father who is in heaven give good things to those who ask Him!*

(Matthew 7:11 NKJV)

# Praying in His Goodness

*Day Three*

# God in a Single Word

*God is love.*
1 John 4:8

If you want to see most clearly what God is really like, all you have to do is study love.

But doesn't the Bible say that God is a jealous God? Doesn't it say that He expects us to worship Him and do things His way by obeying His commands? Yes, but God isn't jealous over us for His own sake. He knows the devil is out there waiting to do us harm and He wants to protect us. He wants us to obey Him because He wants to see us blessed.

That should be easy for us to understand. We're the same way with our own children. For example, we don't tell them to stay out of the street just to prove we are boss. We are trying to help them stay safe so they can live long on the earth and that things will go well with them.

You want your child to obey you because that obedience will open the door for you to bless him. God is not trying to keep us under His thumb by making us worship and obey Him. He is endeavoring to get us in the place where He can safely give us every good and perfect gift.

## Reflecting on His Goodness

What good things does obedience open the door to in a loving
parent-child relationship?

_____

_____

_____

_____

_____

_____

_____

_____

_____

_____

_____

_____

_____

_____

_____

_____

_____

_____

*"Honor your father and your mother," which is the first commandment with promise:*
*"that it may be well with you and you may live long on the earth."*

(Ephesians 6:2–3 NKJV)

## Experiencing His Goodness

Do you tend to relate to God more from a child's perspective or from the mature perspective of a loving parent? List some ways you could start today to view God as a loving parent.

_____

_____

_____

_____

_____

_____

_____

_____

_____

_____

_____

_____

_____

_____

_____

_____

_____

_____

_____

_____

*As a father has compassion on his children, so the LORD has*
*compassion on those who fear him.*

(Psalm 103:13 NIV)

## Praying in His Goodness

*Day Four*

# God Won't Leave You Out

*The LORD hath been mindful of us.*
Psalm 115:12

God's hopes are fadeless where we are concerned. He sees what we can be in Him. You might have walked so far away from God for so long that you think He has forgotten you. But He hasn't.

God thinks about you. Isn't that a blessing? God knows right where you are at all times. You don't have to work to get His attention. He already has you on His mind. He is mindful of His covenant with you. He remembers those things He has promised you, and He knows exactly what it will take to fulfill those promises.

There may be times when you have fallen into disobedience and feel so unworthy that you are tempted to think you are going to be left out of God's blessings. But don't believe that. Remember, the Scripture says if you will call on Him, He will raise you back up into fellowship with Him. Remember it says He is good to *all*. *All* means *every person in existence anywhere*. It guarantees that you will not be left out unless you want to be. If you will reach out to Him in Jesus' name, you will receive from Him.

## Reflecting on His Goodness

How has the world twisted God's "mindfulness" into a negative thing?
How does the fact that God has you on His mind affect you?

_____

_____

_____

_____

_____

_____

_____

_____

_____

_____

_____

_____

_____

_____

_____

_____

_____

_____

*How precious also are thy thoughts unto me, O God! How great is the sum of them!*
*If I should count them, they are more in number than the sand.*

(Psalm 139:17–18)

## Experiencing His Goodness

How do you feel to discover that you don't have to work
to get God's attention?

_____

_____

_____

_____

_____

_____

_____

_____

_____

_____

_____

_____

_____

_____

_____

*[Love] does not rejoice at injustice and unrighteousness, but rejoices when right and
truth prevail. Love bears up under anything and everything that comes, is ever ready
to believe the best of every person; its hopes are fadeless under all circumstances,
and it endures everything [without weakening]. Love never fails.*

(1 Corinthians 13:6–8 AMP)

# Praying in His Goodness

*Day Five*

# You Won't Be Disappointed

*Thou openest thine hand, and satisfiest the desire of every living thing.*
Psalm 145:16

Before now you might have been afraid to make a commitment to God. You might have drawn back from the idea of doing whatever He asked you to do. But now you can make that promise boldly, knowing that whatever He tells you to do will always be for your good.

You will never regret choosing to obey the Lord. Every child of God who has known and trusted His goodness has been eternally glad he did.

The moment you are tempted to draw back in fear from something God tells you to do, remember this: He will only lead you in paths that will ultimately bring you blessing and increase. True, sometimes those paths are not easy. But you can rest assured, they will always take you to good places. In the end, you will find that the difficulties along the road were nothing compared to the reward.

## Reflecting on His Goodness

Why do you think so many verses that speak of God's love,
protection, and blessing use all-inclusive words such as *all* and *every*?
What is God trying to communicate to us?

_____

_____

_____

_____

_____

_____

_____

_____

_____

_____

_____

_____

_____

_____

_____

_____

_____

_____

_____

*The LORD upholdeth all that fall, and raiseth up all those that be bowed down....
The LORD is nigh unto all them that call upon him, to all that call upon him in truth.*

(Psalm 145:14, 18)

## Experiencing His Goodness

Write about a time when you obeyed God without regret. How can
that experience motivate you toward obedience now? What can you
do to commemorate it so that you never forget it?

_____

_____

_____

_____

_____

_____

_____

_____

_____

_____

_____

_____

_____

_____

_____

_____

_____

_____

_____

_____

_____

*[God] Himself has said, I will not in any way fail you nor give you up nor leave you
without support. [I will] not, [I will] not, [I will] not in any degree leave you helpless
nor forsake nor let [you] down (relax My hold on you)!*

(Hebrews 13:5 AMP)

# Praying in His Goodness

## *Tracking God's Goodness Through the Bible*

## *Day One*

## Good from the Beginning

*O give thanks unto the LORD; for he is good: because his mercy endureth for ever.*
Psalm 118:1

If you wish to find out just how much God wants to bless us, all you have to do is read Genesis 1. There we can see God's original intent. He created everything good. He did not create it to be marginal. He did not create it to be just okay. It was a perfect place to live.

When God was finished creating Eden, He saw only one thing that was not good—the fact that man was alone. Do you know what God did when He saw that?

He didn't say, "Now, Adam, I don't want you whining about being alone. I've given you a lot of good things and that ought to be enough." No, that is not His nature! God wanted Adam to be so blessed that there would be nothing lacking in his life. So He fixed the one thing that was not good. He created Eve and gave her to Adam as his wife.

God made every provision and preparation necessary for Adam and Eve to live in perfect blessing. He used His skill and wisdom to plan out the course of their lives and to lead them into every good thing by His benevolent guidance.

## Reflecting on His Goodness

Read Genesis 1–2. How does this account refute the common view that God is stingy? What kind of world did He establish for us?

_____

_____

_____

_____

_____

_____

_____

_____

_____

_____

_____

_____

_____

_____

_____

_____

_____

_____

_____

_____

*And the* LORD *God made all kinds of trees grow out of the ground—trees that were pleasing to the eye and good for food.*

(Genesis 2:9 NIV)

## Experiencing His Goodness

On a scale of one to ten (with one being "nothing" and ten
being "everything"), how much do you ask God for? What holds
you back from asking for more?

---

---

---

---

---

---

---

---

---

---

---

---

---

---

---

---

*Oh, taste and see that the LORD is good; blessed is the man who trusts in Him!*
*Oh, fear the LORD, you His saints! There is no want to those who fear Him.*
*The young lions lack and suffer hunger; but those who seek the LORD*
*shall not lack any good thing.*

(Psalm 34:8–10 NKJV)

# Praying in His Goodness

# Day Two

## The Promise

*I call heaven and earth to record this day against you, that I have set before you life and death, blessing and cursing: therefore choose life, that both thou and thy seed may live: that thou mayest love the LORD thy God, and that thou mayest obey his voice, and that thou mayest cleave unto him: for he is thy life, and the length of thy days.*

Deuteronomy 30:19–20

When most people read the Ten Commandments or the Levitical laws of the Hebrew covenant, they think God gave those laws because He is harsh and demanding. Nothing could be further from the truth!

All mankind had been brought under the curse of sin, and God wanted to provide them a way out. He wanted to give them a way to step back under His protective wing so He could shelter and provide for them once again.

His answer was to send Jesus to bring full, spiritual redemption to the world. But it would take thousands of years for that plan to unfold. God was not willing to wait that long to start blessing His people, so He made a covenant with them, essentially saying, "If you will obey My ways, I will personally take care of all your needs."

Through it all, God spoke to them about the redemption that would be provided through the blood of the Messiah. He gave them the promise of the spiritual deliverance that was to come. He told them that one day there would be a Savior who would pay the price so they could receive a new heart, free from the stain of sin.

## Reflecting on His Goodness

Before now, have you ever thought of God's commands in a positive light? Why or why not? What are you recognizing as their purpose?

_____

_____

_____

_____

_____

_____

_____

_____

_____

_____

_____

_____

_____

_____

_____

_____

_____

_____

_____

_____

_____

*When Christ came as high priest of the good things that are already here, . . . He did not enter by means of the blood of goats and calves; but he entered the Most Holy Place once for all by his own blood, having obtained eternal redemption.*

(Hebrews 9:11–12 NIV)

## Experiencing His Goodness

How difficult is it for you to wait on God's promises to be fulfilled?
What helps you wait on Him?

_If you hearken to these precepts and keep and do them, the Lord your God will keep
with you the covenant and the steadfast love which He swore to your fathers.
And He will love you, bless you, and multiply you._

(Deuteronomy 7:12–13 AMP)

# Praying in His Goodness

# Day Three

## Our Long-suffering God

*I am the LORD thy God which teacheth thee to profit, which leadeth thee by the way that thou shouldest go. O that thou hadst hearkened to my commandments! Then had thy peace been as a river, and thy righteousness as the waves of the sea.*

Isaiah 48:17–18

Even when the Israelites in Jeremiah's time blatantly said to God once and for all, "We are not going to do what You tell us to do," God refused to give up on them. In His goodness and long-suffering, He would not quit.

As they went into captivity, God already had a plan in motion to gather them back to their land and bring them once again into the place of His promised blessing.

Think about all God had been through with those disobedient people! They had turned their backs on Him for forty years. They had rejected the God who wanted only to do them good. Any human being would have washed his hands of a people like that. But God's compassions are new every morning. He still wanted good for His people. He still wanted them to be free. He still wanted to lavish His mercy upon them.

Do you see how good God is? Even when His people have rebelled against Him again and again, He looks forward to the time when they return to Him. He gets joy when they do what He says so that He can freely come into their lives and do them good!

## Reflecting on His Goodness

Does the long-suffering of God surprise you, especially in light of Israel's decades of rebellion? Explain.

_____

_____

_____

_____

_____

_____

_____

_____

_____

_____

_____

_____

_____

_____

_____

_____

_____

_____

_____

_____

*The Lord is not slack concerning His promise, as some count slackness, but is longsuffering toward us, not willing that any should perish but that all should come to repentance.*

(2 Peter 3:9 NKJV)

# Experiencing His Goodness

In what area of your life has God's patience been most evident? What have you done with that merciful gift?

_____

_____

_____

_____

_____

_____

_____

_____

_____

_____

_____

_____

_____

_____

_____

_____

_____

_____

_____

_____

_____

*This I recall to my mind, therefore have I hope. It is of the LORD's mercies that we are not consumed, because his compassions fail not. They are new every morning: great is thy faithfulness.*

(Lamentations 3:21–23)

# Praying in His Goodness

## Day Four

## Understanding God's Heart

*O Jerusalem, Jerusalem, ... How often I have desired and yearned to gather
your children together [around Me], as a hen [gathers] her young under her
wings, but you would not!*

Luke 13:34 AMP

Although God's merciful attitude toward the Israelites is amazing, it is not
unusual. Read the entire Bible and you will find He was always this way with
His people. Why? Because that's His heart.

Over and over again, He would give them His Word. Over and over again,
they would disobey it and suffer the painful consequences. Yet God never
looked at His people when they were in trouble and said, "I'm glad they're
hurting. They're just getting what they deserve!" No, His heart longed for
them just as our hearts long for our children when we see them getting into
trouble and suffering because of it. He longed for them to obey Him because
He knew if they would, they could live free and victorious.

Because we didn't know God's heart, there have been times in our lives
when we've felt God didn't care about us. We had unmet needs, so we thought
He had neglected us. But it was the other way around. He was always ready to
supply our needs. We just were not in a position to receive.

God loves every person, but He is only obligated to the welfare of the person who receives Him into his life by believing and obeying His covenant.

## Reflecting on His Goodness

The apostle Paul's story reveals the goodness of God in some
powerful ways. Read it in Acts 22:3–21, noting all that God did
to draw this murderer of His people to Himself.

_____

_____

_____

_____

_____

_____

_____

_____

_____

_____

_____

_____

_____

_____

_____

_____

_____

_____

*I will bless the LORD at all times; His praise shall continually be in my mouth.... This
poor man cried out, and the LORD heard him, and saved him out of all his troubles.
The angel of the LORD encamps all around those who fear Him, and delivers them.*

(Psalm 34:1, 6–7 NKJV)

## Experiencing His Goodness

What are some things God has done to draw you to Himself in the past? What is He doing right now to bring you closer to Him?

_____

_____

_____

_____

_____

_____

_____

_____

_____

_____

_____

_____

_____

_____

_____

_____

_____

_____

_____

*The man who looks intently into the perfect law that gives freedom, and continues to do this, not forgetting what he has heard, but doing it—he will be blessed in what he does.*

(James 1:25 NIV)

# Praying in His Goodness

# The Perfect Picture of God

*[God's Son] is the sole expression of the glory of God ... the perfect
imprint and very image of [God's] nature.*
Hebrews 1:3 AMP

The best and most perfect revelation of God's goodness comes to us in
the New Testament through His Son, Jesus. He is the fullest expression of the
Father's heart. He is the fulfillment of the Hebrew covenant.

Jesus so embodies the character and nature of God that everything He
said and did while He was on the earth was an expression of the will of God.
Therefore, if we want to know what God desires to do for us today, all we have
to do is see what He did for people while He was on the earth.

Jesus went about doing good because God is a good God. When He saw
people were physically hungry, He didn't just turn His back and say, "Well,
they'll be okay. They ought to be fasting more anyway." No, He worked a
miracle in order to feed them. It was the Father's will.

When people were spiritually hungry, He taught them. When people
were sick and they came to Him, He healed them. When they asked, He even
went to them.

Jesus demonstrated to us that God wants to meet the needs of all who
come to Him in faith.

## Reflecting on His Goodness

Read the following accounts of Jesus' ministry: Matthew 4:23–24,
8:1–3, 14:13–19; Luke 18:15–16. What do they say about God's heart?

_____

_____

_____

_____

_____

_____

_____

_____

_____

_____

_____

_____

_____

_____

_____

_____

_____

_____

*Anyone who has seen Me has seen the Father.*

(John 14:9 AMP)

## Experiencing His Goodness

At the wedding feast in Cana (John 2:1–11), Jesus stepped in to meet even a seemingly insignificant need. What are some noneternal needs you've had that God has responded to when you've asked? How much more do you think He must care about your deepest needs?

_____

_____

_____

_____

_____

_____

_____

_____

_____

_____

_____

_____

_____

_____

_____

_____

_____

_____

_____

*God anointed Jesus of Nazareth with the Holy Ghost and with power:*
*who went about doing good, and healing all that were oppressed of the devil;*
*for God was with him.*

(Acts 10:38)

# Praying in His Goodness

*Blessings Stored Up for You*

*Day One*

## An Ocean of Goodness

*But as it is written, Eye hath not seen, nor ear heard, neither have entered into the heart of man, the things which God hath prepared for them that love him.*

1 Corinthians 2:9

God is absolutely unlimited in His ability and His resources. And He is unlimited in His desire to pour out those resources upon us. We know of nothing that delights Him more than the opportunity to give blessings to His obedient children from His abundance.

One description of God's boundless capacity and desire to give comes from F. F. Bosworth's book, *Christ the Healer.* It says: "Imagine that the vast Pacific Ocean was elevated high above us. Then imagine it poured out and pressing into every crevice to find an outlet through which it might stream its flood tides over all the earth, and you have a picture of God's benevolent attitude toward us" (Whitaker House, 2000, p. 78).

Just imagine that! An ocean of God's goodness stored up just waiting to be poured out in our lives!

## Reflecting on His Goodness

In what ways do we limit God's blessings? Why is it so hard to believe that He wants to pour out goodness in our lives?

_____

_____

_____

_____

_____

_____

_____

_____

_____

_____

_____

_____

_____

_____

_____

_____

_____

_____

_____

_____

_____

_____

*God . . . giveth us richly all things to enjoy.*

(1 Timothy 6:17)

## Experiencing His Goodness

The limitations of God's goodness are on the human side. There are no limits on the divine side. Understanding that, what can you start doing today to quit limiting God in your life?

_____

_____

_____

_____

_____

_____

_____

_____

_____

_____

_____

_____

_____

_____

_____

_____

_____

_____

*The LORD . . . takes pleasure in the prosperity of His servant.*

(Psalm 35:27 AMP)

# Praying in His Goodness

# Day Two

## God Is Good... All the Time

*Now we have not received the spirit [that belongs to] the world, but the [Holy] Spirit Who is from God, [given to us] that we might realize and comprehend and appreciate the gifts [of divine favor and blessing so freely and lavishly] bestowed on us by God.*
1 Corinthians 2:12 AMP

God is good in the Old Testament... and God is good in the New Testament. The New Testament written after the Messiah came is just the next step in fulfilling God's plan of redemption. Our covenant includes all the promises of natural provision made by the old, plus the spiritual blessings of the new birth, freedom from sin, and the baptism in the Holy Spirit—and all of it is ours right now!

You and I will never be able to see with our natural eyes and hear with our natural ears the whole truth about the goodness of God and His benefits. It has to enter our hearts through the wisdom of God that comes to us by His Spirit and His Word. The Holy Spirit speaks it to our hearts, and then it comes into our minds and we begin to see the wonderful things God has laid up and keeps ready for us.

Think of it! Everything you need has already been prepared by God, and it is ready and waiting for all who qualify for this scriptural promise! Who qualifies? "Them that love him."

## Reflecting on His Goodness

What difference does it make that God is always the same God throughout Scripture and throughout the course of human history?

---

---

---

---

---

---

---

---

---

---

---

---

---

---

---

---

---

---

---

---

---

---

---

---

---

*I am the LORD, I change not.*

(Malachi 3:6)

## Experiencing His Goodness

What does "loving God" look like? See Micah 6:8 and John 14:21 to
get you started, then add your own ideas.

_____

_____

_____

_____

_____

_____

_____

_____

_____

_____

_____

_____

_____

_____

_____

_____

_____

_____

_____

_____

_____

*Be very careful . . . to love the LORD your God, to walk in all his ways, to obey his
commands, to hold fast to him and to serve him with all your heart and all your soul.*

(Joshua 22:5 NIV)

# Praying in His Goodness

## Day Three

## Here and Now

*Oh how great is thy goodness, which thou hast laid up for them that fear thee; which thou hast wrought for them that trust in thee before the sons of men!*
Psalm 31:19

It is true that there are wonderful, heavenly rewards that are awaiting you after you pass over. But there are vast earthly blessings ready for you to receive now in this life.

Hebrews 1:14 calls us as New Covenant believers "heirs of salvation." Most people think salvation simply provides them entrance into heaven when they die. The full definition of the Greek word *soteria* denotes "deliverance, preservation, material and temporal deliverance from danger and apprehension, pardon, protection, liberty, health, restoration, soundness and wholeness." Salvation includes everything in your life you could ever need—whether it is eternal security in heaven or a car to drive on earth. It includes healing for your body and a home for your family.

That's your inheritance! And it comes to you through faith in Jesus as the Lord of your life. No wonder the angels said at His birth, "Peace on earth, good will toward men!" They understood that He was going to unlock the treasure house of God's goodness and make it available to all people everywhere. They knew that Jesus was going to obtain the whole package of salvation through His life, death, and resurrection.

They knew just how much that meant.

## Reflecting on His Goodness

According to Hebrews 11:6, what role does faith play in our salvation and blessing?

_____

_____

_____

_____

_____

_____

_____

_____

_____

_____

_____

_____

_____

_____

_____

_____

_____

_____

_____

*When the kindness and love of God our Savior appeared, he saved us, not because of righteous things we had done, but because of his mercy.*

(Titus 3:4–5 NIV)

## Experiencing His Goodness

In light of God's promises to His heirs, let your imagination run
wild. What would be the best thing you can imagine God doing or
preparing specifically for you in the here and now?

_____

_____

_____

_____

_____

_____

_____

_____

_____

_____

_____

_____

_____

_____

_____

_____

_____

_____

_____

_____

_____

*Every beast of the forest is Mine, and the cattle on a thousand hills. . . . If I were
hungry, I would not tell you; for the world is Mine, and all its fullness.*
(Psalm 50:10, 12 NKJV)

# Praying in His Goodness

# Day Four

## God's Tenderness Toward "Thomases"

*I will make all my goodness pass before thee, and I will proclaim
the name of the LORD before thee.*
Exodus 33:19

Sometimes people think God just expects them to believe what the Bible says about Him, and if they don't, tough luck; He won't have anything to do with them. But the fact is, if someone sincerely wants to believe in Him but he is struggling with doubts and misunderstandings, God is willing to help him by revealing Himself.

That is what He did for "doubting Thomas." The other disciples reported to him that Jesus had been raised from the dead. But Thomas couldn't bring himself to believe it. How did Jesus respond? By showing him what he wanted to see.

As believers, we don't need to have signs and wonders to convince us God's Word is true. We already know and we are to stand fast in faith on what we know. But others, who have not yet been blessed with the revelation we have, are going to receive help from God. He will show them something to help them believe!

I am convinced He wants to use the outpouring of His goodness in our lives as one way to do it.

## Reflecting on His Goodness

Check out the story of the father whose son had an evil spirit in
Mark 9:17–24. Have you ever shared the father's plea in verse 24?
How did God respond?

_____

_____

_____

_____

_____

_____

_____

_____

_____

_____

_____

_____

_____

_____

_____

_____

_____

*Oh, that men would give thanks to the* LORD *for His goodness, and for
His wonderful works . . . ! For He satisfies the longing soul, and fills
the hungry soul with goodness.*

(Psalm 107:8–9 NKJV)

## Experiencing His Goodness

What is your biggest question for God—something you think you may not be understanding but desperately want answered? Ask Him here for His help, even if that means learning to accept a different answer (or no answer this side of heaven).

_____

_____

_____

_____

_____

_____

_____

_____

_____

_____

_____

_____

_____

_____

_____

_____

_____

_____

*Because you have seen me, you have believed. Blessed are those who*
*have not seen and yet have believed.*

(Mark 20:29 NIV)

# Praying in His Goodness

*Day Five*

# Living Memorials of God's Goodness

*And [Jerusalem] shall be to Me a name of joy, a praise, and a glory before*
*all the nations of the earth that hear of all the good I do for it.*

Jeremiah 33:9 AMP

One reason we need to prosper and be in victory is to show people around us that God is good. The word *show* means "to boldly stand out opposite, certify, declare, plainly profess, report, show forth, speak." God wants His people to stand out boldly opposite so that others can see that there is a God in heaven. He wants to tell the world something through the lives of His people. He wants to tell them He's a good God!

Then it should not surprise us that God wants us to be so blessed that we are memorials, too. He wants our lives overflowing with good. He wants people to look at us and see we are different. We are not worried. We are not depressed. We are prosperous when the economy is up and when it is down. Nothing seems to take us off our path. We just keep going on our way, blessed and full of the joy of the Lord.

One of the most powerful evangelistic tools we have is the manifestation of the goodness of God in our lives and the joy that goodness brings. People are hungry for goodness. They are hungry for joy. I believe it's time we showed it to them. Don't you?

# Reflecting on His Goodness

What should the world see in God's people? They should see
the blessing of God!

_____

_____

_____

_____

_____

_____

_____

_____

_____

_____

_____

_____

_____

_____

_____

_____

_____

_____

_____

_____

_____

*[They are living memorials] to show that the Lord is upright and*
*faithful to His promises.*

(Psalm 92:15 AMP)

## Experiencing His Goodness

What messages has the world been getting about God's goodness and power as they've watched you living your life? Brainstorm some ways you can be an ever better "living memorial."

_____

_____

_____

_____

_____

_____

_____

_____

_____

_____

_____

_____

_____

_____

_____

_____

_____

_____

_____

*To me, . . . this grace was given, that I should preach among the Gentiles the unsearchable riches of Christ.*

(Ephesians 3:8 NKJV)

# Praying in His Goodness

*A Good Plan and a Good Place*

*Day One*

## A Place Just for You

*The earth is the Lord's, and the fullness of it, the world and they who dwell in it.*
Psalm 24:1 AMP

God has a good place for you, a specific spot on this physical earth that He has prepared especially for you.

That may surprise you. Like many people, you may believe that God is so heavenly minded, He doesn't care about your natural surroundings. But I believe, in His providence, God has provided His every son and daughter a blessed and peaceful place that is theirs to inhabit and enjoy!

Read the Bible and you will see that land has always been important to God. He created it and it belongs to Him. Even though He owns it, He does not need it for Himself. He created it for His family so they would have a place to enjoy their life and fellowship with Him.

Of course, the entrance of sin into the earth created a different environment, but it did not change God's desire and heart. He wanted Adam and Eve to have a good place to live, and He wants us to have a good place to live.

Just keep walking in the ways of the Lord and trusting His goodness. He has a garden just for you.

## Reflecting on His Goodness

Why would God give us beautiful surroundings and not just practical ones? What function does beauty serve?

_____

_____

_____

_____

_____

_____

_____

_____

_____

_____

_____

_____

_____

_____

_____

_____

_____

_____

_____

_____

_____

_____

*The desert shall rejoice and blossom as the rose; it shall blossom abundantly and rejoice. . . . They shall see the glory of the LORD, the excellency of our God.*

(Isaiah 35:1–2 NKJV)

## Experiencing His Goodness

What is it about nature that speaks to you? In your mind's eye, how does it manifest the goodness of the Lord?

_____

_____

_____

_____

_____

_____

_____

_____

_____

_____

_____

_____

_____

_____

_____

_____

_____

_____

_____

_____

_____

*Who is the man that fears the LORD? Him shall He teach in the way He chooses. He himself shall dwell in prosperity, and his descendants shall inherit the earth.*

(Psalm 25:12–13 NKJV)

# Praying in His Goodness

# Day Two

## Prepared Paths

*We are God's [own] handiwork (His workmanship), recreated in Christ Jesus, [born anew] that we may do those good works which God predestined (planned beforehand) for us [taking paths which He prepared ahead of time], that we should walk in them [living the good life which He prearranged and made ready for us to live].*

Ephesians 2:10 AMP

You are God's handiwork. You are divinely designed to fulfill the good destiny God has planned for you.

When you were born, God placed certain abilities, dreams, and desires within you that would help equip you for what He wanted you to do. Even before you gave your life to Him, while you were still a sinner, they were there.

So even before you knowingly begin to seek God, He already has a plan working for you. He has already given you some equipment that will help you walk out that plan. You may not recognize its true value before you give your life to Him because your understanding will be limited. Without His Word and His Spirit to enlighten you, you can never grasp the full plan God has for you.

That is why those of us who know the Lord want to share the gospel with every creature! We want everyone to have the opportunity to live out God's wonderful plan right here on earth and into eternity!

## Reflecting on His Goodness

There are Christians who take the first step into God's plan by making Jesus the Lord of their lives, but that's as far as they go. What else do they need to experience the fullness of God in their life? What role does the Holy Spirit play?

_____

_____

_____

_____

_____

_____

_____

_____

_____

_____

_____

_____

_____

_____

_____

_____

_____

_____

*All this I have spoken while still with you. But the Counselor, the Holy Spirit,*
*whom the Father will send in my name, will teach you all things and remind*
*you of everything I have said to you.*

(John 14:25–26 NIV)

## Experiencing His Goodness

What do you think may be God's plan for you? How has He equipped you? Identify some ways you can start to pursue His plan this week . . . this month . . . this year.

_____

_____

_____

_____

_____

_____

_____

_____

_____

_____

_____

_____

_____

_____

_____

_____

_____

_____

_____

*"For I know the plans I have for you," declares the* LORD, *"plans to prosper you and not to harm you, plans to give you hope and a future."*
(Jeremiah 29:11 NIV)

## Praying in His Goodness

*Day Three*

## God's Trustworthy Timetable

*We are assured and know that [God being a partner in their labor] all things work together and are [fitting into a plan] for good to and for those who love God and are called according to [His] design and purpose.*

Romans 8:28 AMP

Part of God's goodness is that He is a planner. And what a planner! He mapped out the plan of redemption before the foundation of the world (Rev. 13:8). When man sinned, that plan was in place. He already has the plan for the new heaven and new earth.

Everything God has planned for the earth will come to pass right on time. Jesus was born at the appointed time. He was crucified and raised from the dead at the appointed time, and He is coming back at the appointed time. He won't be one day late.

In light of these facts, consider this: the same good God who planned those events is the One who planned your life. When you were born again, He equipped you with the ability to hear His voice and obey Him in all things. He made you into a new creature who can walk in His power and wisdom. He has made you to be victorious. He filled you with Himself to give you power to fulfill His plan. He has wonderful plans, high hopes, and great faith for your future because He knows what you can do—with His help, of course!

## Reflecting on His Goodness

We have a right-on-time God. When have you seen evidence of this in your life? What further biblical evidence can you point to?

_____

_____

_____

_____

_____

_____

_____

_____

_____

_____

_____

_____

_____

_____

_____

_____

_____

_____

_____

_____

_____

*Then the LORD said to Abraham, ". . . Is anything too hard for [me]? I will return to you at the appointed time next year and Sarah will have a son."*

(GENESIS 18:13–14 NIV)

## Experiencing His Goodness

What will worry do to your ability to hear and act on the Lord's plan?
How important is it to follow His timetable?

_____

_____

_____

_____

_____

_____

_____

_____

_____

_____

_____

_____

_____

_____

_____

_____

_____

_____

_____

*The LORD longs to be gracious to you; he rises to show you compassion....*
*Blessed are all who wait for him!*

(Isaiah 30:18 NIV)

## Praying in His Goodness

## Day Four

## It's Not Too Late

*While he was still a long way off, his father saw him and was filled with compassion*
*for him; he ran to his son, threw his arms around him and kissed him.*
Luke 15:20 NIV

Maybe you walked with God in the past and experienced some of His plan for your life, but you were drawn away from Him by some sinful bait the devil offered. You may feel like the country gospel singer who sang, "I got what I wanted but I lost what I had."

If so, let me tell you, you are not the first to go astray. A lot of people have sold out their freedom and their lives with God for something out there in the world. But even if you have done that, you can be like the prodigal son in the Bible. You can turn around and go home. When you do, God's mercy will be right there to greet you. He will say, "Welcome home, son. Welcome home, daughter." He will put a robe of righteousness on your back and bring you into that place He has prepared for you because He is good and His mercy endures forever!

## Reflecting on His Goodness

Not all prodigals squander wealth. What else do we waste
when we stray from God?

---

*Oh, that they had such a heart in them that they would . . . always keep all My
commandments, that it might be well with them and with their children forever!*

(Deuteronomy 5:29 NKJV)

## Experiencing His Goodness

Have you ever been drawn away from God's plan for your life? What brought you back? How tempting is that same distraction today? Explain.

_Look to the LORD and his strength; seek His face evermore!_
(Psalm 105:4 NKJV)

# Praying in His Goodness

## Nothing Compares with His Plan

*Then shall ye call upon me, and ye shall go and pray unto me, and I will hearken unto you. And ye shall seek me, and find me, when ye shall search for me with all your heart. And I will be found of you, saith the LORD.*
Jeremiah 29:12–14

God is always drawing you into His plan. That's why I believe you ought to get up first thing every morning and tune in to Him through prayer and Bible reading. He knows where you need to be. He knows what you need to do each day to stay on track. He knows the plan! Seek Him and you will see it, too.

There may be times when you get to a plateau and don't seem to be going anywhere. When that happens, just dive into His Word in greater measure and ask Him to show you where you've missed it. We all have to step back and regroup sometimes; we miss God's direction now and then. But as we continue obeying the promptings of His Spirit, God will draw us deeper and deeper into His plan.

I don't care what you've been doing until now; if you haven't been in the plan of God, you haven't done anything yet. You may have material riches but, even so, you will never experience true prosperity until you step into what God has planned.

## Reflecting on His Goodness

Even spiritually mature people must continually follow the inward witness of the Spirit to stay on God's path. Give God attention!

_____

_____

_____

_____

_____

_____

_____

_____

_____

_____

_____

_____

_____

_____

_____

_____

_____

_____

_____

*Through wisdom is an house builded; and by understanding it is established: and by knowledge shall the chambers be filled with all precious and pleasant riches.*

(Proverbs 24:3–4)

## Experiencing His Goodness

Have you ever believed God was calling you to do things you didn't think you could do? How did you respond? What will you do next time He invites you to step out of your comfort zone?

_____

_____

_____

_____

_____

_____

_____

_____

_____

_____

_____

_____

_____

_____

_____

_____

_____

_____

_____

*If any of you lack wisdom, let him ask of God, that giveth to all men liberally, and upbraideth not; and it shall be given him.*

(James 1:5)

# Praying in His Goodness

*Enjoying God's Best*

## Day One

## Two Kingdoms

*[The Father] has delivered and drawn us to Himself out of the control and the dominion of darkness and has transferred us into the kingdom of the Son of His love.*
Colossians 1:13 AMP

Whenever the subject of God's goodness is discussed, one question will invariably arise: "If God is so good, why is there so much evil and pain in the world?"

The answer is actually quite simple. God is not the only one at work in the earth. There is another spiritual being who constantly opposes Him. The one who opposes Him is the source of all evil. His name is Satan. Also known as the devil.

One day the devil and all who serve him will be totally removed from the earth. In that day, things will be as God intended them to be in the beginning. Until that time, however, there will continue to be two kingdoms operating here.

The moment we believe in and confess Jesus, we are released from the laws of the devil's kingdom, and we come instead under a completely new government ruled by a higher law. Where Satan's law of sin and death brought us bondage and destruction, the law of the Spirit of life in Christ Jesus brings us freedom and restoration. Where the law of sin and death brought the curse, the law of the Spirit of life brings the blessing.

# Reflecting on His Goodness

In the parable in Matthew 12:24–30, what are the two kingdoms compared to? Why are these descriptions appropriate?

_____

_____

_____

_____

_____

_____

_____

_____

_____

_____

_____

_____

_____

_____

_____

_____

_____

_____

_____

_____

*For the law of the Spirit of life [which is] in Christ Jesus [the law of our new being] has freed me from the law of sin and of death.*

(Romans 8:2 AMP)

## Experiencing His Goodness

Instead of operating by fear, the kingdom of God operates on faith.
Which realm do you spend more time in? What are the results?

_____

_____

_____

_____

_____

_____

_____

_____

_____

_____

_____

_____

_____

_____

_____

_____

_____

_____

_____

*I beseech you therefore, brethren, by the mercies of God, that ye present your bodies a living sacrifice, holy, acceptable unto God, which is your reasonable service. And be not conformed to this world: but be ye transformed by the renewing of your mind, that ye may prove what is that good, and acceptable, and perfect, will of God.*

(Romans 12:1–2)

# Praying in His Goodness

## Day Two

## Your Way, or His?

*"I have set before you life and death, blessing and cursing; therefore choose life, that both you and your descendants may live; that you may love the LORD your God, that you may obey His voice, and that you may cling to Him, for He is your life."*
Deuteronomy 30:19–20 NKJV

Unlike the devil, who tries to dominate those in his kingdom on every hand, God makes the people in His kingdom free. He is not a dictator. He does not force us to do His will. He does not even force us to live our lives by His operating principles. If we want to, we may submit ourselves again to the bondage of darkness, or we can walk in His liberty and light. It's our choice. Freedom to choose is a gift of God. When you cling to Him, He clings to you.

If we choose to live His way and submit ourselves to the law of the Spirit of life in Christ Jesus, we will experience blessing. If we choose to live the devil's way and submit again to the bondage of sin and death, we will experience the curse. That's the law! You do not have a choice whether or not you live under spiritual law. It is like the law of gravity. It functions. However, you do get to choose which law: the law of life or the law of death.

# Reflecting on His Goodness

What are some of the means by which God tries to reach people so that they will choose the way of life?

_____

_____

_____

_____

_____

_____

_____

_____

_____

_____

_____

_____

_____

_____

_____

_____

_____

_____

_____

_____

_____

*Come close to God and He will come close to you.*

(James 4:8 AMP)

## Experiencing His Goodness

If not yet, someday you will be faced with a choice similar to Joshua's in Joshua 24:15 where Joshua said to the people of Israel, "Choose today whom you will serve." How can you be readying yourself now to choose wisely when the time comes?

---

*You are great in counsel and mighty in work, for your eyes are open to all the ways of the sons of men, to give everyone according to his ways and according to the fruit of his doings.*

(Jeremiah 32:19 NKJV)

# Praying in His Goodness

*Day Three*

## Surrounded by Goodness

*Where is the man who fears the Lord? God will teach him how to choose the best.*
*He shall live within God's circle of blessing.*
Psalm 25:12–13 TLB

Did you know that you can have a faith class anytime you want? Did you know you can tune in to the teaching of the Holy Spirit any hour of the day or night and find out what God wants you to do because He is living in your heart?

Once we gave our lives to Him, God not only made His written Word available to us, He put His own Holy Spirit in our hearts to teach us exactly how to apply that Word to our lives.

We are a blessed people! We have the Lord Himself to teach us His ways. If we will walk in those ways when God shows them to us, we will "dwell in prosperity" (Psalm 25:13). That's a wonderful place to live, don't you think? What's more, I can take that blessed environment with me wherever I go! It's not tied to a particular location. It's not tied to circumstances. It's in my heart and my relationship with the Lord. God's goodness surrounds me wherever I go.

# Reflecting on His Goodness

What's wrong with the world's wisdom? Why doesn't it make sense in the kingdom of God?

_____

_____

_____

_____

_____

_____

_____

_____

_____

_____

_____

_____

_____

_____

_____

*No one knows the thoughts of God except the Spirit of God.... This is what we speak, not in words taught us by human wisdom but in words taught by the Spirit, expressing spiritual truths in spiritual words.*

(1 Corinthians 2:11, 13 NIV)

## Experiencing His Goodness

How has the Holy Spirit opened to you the mind of Christ
and the words of God? What is different about the way
you read, understand, and apply Scripture?

_____

_____

_____

_____

_____

_____

_____

_____

_____

_____

_____

_____

_____

_____

_____

_____

_____

_____

_____

_____

*Good and upright is the LORD; therefore He teaches sinners in the way. The humble*
*He guides in justice, and the humble He teaches His way.*

(Psalm 25:8–9 NKJV)

# Praying in His Goodness

# Day Four

## Resisting the Enemy

*I have told you these things, so that in Me you may have [perfect] peace and confidence.
In the world you have tribulation and trials and distress and frustration; but be of good
cheer [take courage; be confident, certain, undaunted]! For I have overcome the world.*

John 16:33 AMP

Not every Christian who runs into trouble is somehow in disobedience
to the Lord. There are wonderful believers who love the Lord and live good,
godly lives and yet they experience tragic things.

The Bible does not say you will not have any trouble, but it does say over
and over that God will bring you out of trouble. It also says, "The just shall
live by faith" (Rom. 1:17). When trouble comes, faith in God's Word will bring
victory.

We have an enemy. He comes to steal, kill, and destroy. We have authority
over him in the name of Jesus, but even so, he will challenge us to see if we will
really use that authority against him.

Although we enjoy a great deal of protection from him simply by avoid-
ing sin and living in obedience to the Word of God, we have to be spiritually
aggressive. If we want to enjoy all the blessings of God's kingdom, we have to
find out what they are and then take hold of them by faith and receive them.
What God offers has to be received. And when the devil tries to take those
blessings away, we must resist him.

# Reflecting on His Goodness

Look up the following passages that describe Satan: John 8:44, 10:10;
1 John 5:18; 1 Peter 5:8; Revelation 12:9–10. What insight do
these verses give you into his nature and his ways?

_____

_____

_____

_____

_____

_____

_____

_____

_____

_____

_____

_____

_____

_____

_____

_____

_____

*Whatsoever is born of God overcometh the world: and this is the victory that
overcometh the world, even our faith.*

(1 John 5:4)

## Experiencing His Goodness

When has Satan attacked your life of faith? What helps you
withstand his attacks? How well are you using your armor
and your sword, which is the Word of God, both
offensively and defensively (Eph. 6:14–18)?

_____

_____

_____

_____

_____

_____

_____

_____

_____

_____

_____

_____

_____

_____

_____

_____

_____

_____

_____

_____

_____

_____

_____

*Finally, my brethren, be strong in the Lord and in the power of His might. Put on the
whole armor of God, that you may be able to stand against the wiles of the devil.*

(Ephesians 6:10–11 NKJV)

# Praying in His Goodness

*Day Five*

## Anytime, Anyplace, in Any Situation

*Thou shalt not be afraid for the terror by night; nor for the arrow that flieth by day; nor for the pestilence that walketh in darkness; nor for the destruction that wasteth at noonday. A thousand shall fall at thy side, and ten thousand at thy right hand; but it shall not come nigh thee.*
Psalm 91:5–7

Because they don't understand how much spiritual things affect this natural earth, most people assume the results in their lives are determined by their natural environment, resources, and circumstances. But the truth is, the blessings (or lack of them) in our lives are determined by the spiritual kingdom in which we are operating.

If you are a citizen of the kingdom of God, all things are possible to you no matter where you live. God is not dependent on governments and methods of men. He will intervene and use those things, but He is not restricted by them. He has the power to get you what you need anytime, anyplace, and in any situation.

When God's kingdom comes on the scene, even natural, worldly systems begin to work in favor of the believer. If you'll honor and obey Him, you can live in the light of His goodness right in the midst of a dark world. You will begin to experience increase. In a world plagued by shortages and lack, you'll find He is able to "supply all your need according to his riches in glory by Christ Jesus" (Philippians 4:19).

# Reflecting on His Goodness

Where does Psalm 91 tell us is the safest place on earth for those who abide in God? What are the ways He protects us, according to this passage?

_____

_____

_____

_____

_____

_____

_____

_____

_____

_____

_____

_____

_____

_____

_____

_____

_____

*Bless the LORD, O my soul: and all that is within me, bless his holy name. Bless the LORD, O my soul, and forget not all his benefits: who forgiveth all thine iniquities; who healeth all thy diseases; who redeemeth thy life from destruction; who crowneth thee with lovingkindness and tender mercies.*

(Psalm 103:1–4)

## Experiencing His Goodness

There is a song, inspired by Isaiah 53:1–6, that asks, "Whose report will you believe?" and responds: "I shall believe the report of the Lord!" Are you being tempted right now to believe another person's report instead of God's—the words of a doctor? a boss? a family member? Write a true "report" from the Psalms that you can begin to commit to memory.

*We walk by faith, not by sight.*
(2 Corinthians 5:7)

# Praying in His Goodness

## The Key to Heaven's Storehouse

## Day One

## First Things First

*But seek ye first the kingdom of God, and his righteousness; and all these
things shall be added unto you.*
Matthew 6:33

Once we realize God has a storehouse of good things laid up for us and
we decide to plant ourselves firmly in His kingdom so that we qualify for
those blessings, the first question we want to ask is this: what can I do to
open the door to God's storehouse so I can begin receiving the things God
has for me?

In Matthew 6:24–33 Jesus tells us that God's way to gain natural provision
and prosperity is as different from the worldly way as day is from night. The
world teaches us to make material wealth our goal. It teaches us to focus on
and pursue the money we need to buy the things we want. But God instructs
us to do just the opposite.

He tells us not to focus on material riches. Instead, seek Him first and trust
Him to supply your needs. He says in essence, *Don't push and strive to gain material
riches for yourself. Serve Me and I'll give them to you.*

In other words, God is our source.

# Reflecting on His Goodness

When we spend all our time striving for material wealth, what are we in effect saying about God?

_____

_____

_____

_____

_____

_____

_____

_____

_____

_____

_____

_____

_____

_____

_____

_____

_____

_____

*Consider the lilies of the field, how they grow: they neither toil nor spin; and yet I say to you that even Solomon in all his glory was not arrayed like one of these. Now if God so clothes the grass of the field, which today is, and tomorrow is thrown into the oven, will He not much more clothe you, O you of little faith? Therefore do not worry, saying, "What shall we eat?" or "What shall we drink?" or "What shall we wear?" . . . For your heavenly Father knows that you need all these things.*

(Matthew 6:28–32 NKJV)

# Experiencing His Goodness

When you have a need, is God your first choice, your "plan B,"
or more of a last resort? What holds you back from
relying on Him more?

*The LORD is my shepherd; I shall not want. He maketh me to lie down in green
pastures: he leadeth me beside the still waters.... Surely goodness and mercy shall
follow me all the days of my life: and I will dwell in the house of the LORD for ever.*

(Psalm 23:1–2, 6)

## Praying in His Goodness

*Day Two*

## Diligence: The Next Level

*And it shall come to pass, if thou shalt hearken diligently unto the voice of the
LORD thy God, to observe and to do all his commandments which I command thee
this day, that the LORD thy God will set thee on high above all nations of the earth:
and all these blessings shall come on thee, and overtake thee, if thou shalt hearken
unto the voice of the LORD thy God.*

Deuteronomy 28:1–2

Seeking God is not a onetime event. It's a lifestyle of going after God and
His ways—researching God and His ways in order to obey them.

In addition to spending time with the Lord in prayer and feeding your
spirit with His Word, you put God first by taking one day at a time and living
for God. You do what He shows you to do that day. You listen to the Holy
Spirit. When situations arise and you have a choice either to handle them
God's way or the world's way, you choose God's way.

Obedience is required in putting God first place in your life. When you
seek God first, you let Him be God in every area of your life. You give yourself to Him out of honor, reverence, and love. You make a decision: "All right,
Lord, I'll do whatever You tell me to do. I'm giving You the rest of my days on
this earth—starting today." Then you let God be God in your life.

He's the first One you believe. He's the first One you obey.

## Reflecting on His Goodness

When does any pursuit transition from being an interest to a lifestyle?
Why is it important to continuously seek God?

*The LORD is good . . . to the soul that seeketh him.*

(Lamentations 3:25)

## Experiencing His Goodness

Replace the word *seek* (or its variation) with the word *research* in each of these verses (KJV): 1 Chronicles 16:11; Isaiah 55:6; Psalm 9:10, 34:4, 69:32. How does this exercise expand your understanding of what you need to do in your pursuit of God's kingdom?

*Man shall not live by bread alone, but by every word that proceedeth out of the mouth of God.*

(Matthew 4:4)

# Praying in His Goodness

*Day Three*

## Our Passionate Pursuit

*One thing have I asked of the Lord, that will I seek, inquire for, and [insistently] require: that I may dwell in the house of the Lord [in His presence] all the days of my life, to behold and gaze upon the beauty [the sweet attractiveness and the delightful loveliness] of the Lord and to meditate, consider, and inquire in His temple.*

Psalm 27:4 AMP

Real seekers don't just go after the things of God casually, when it's convenient. They go after Him as if they cannot live without Him. They seek Him, as *The Amplified Bible* says, out of "vital necessity" (1 Chronicles 22:19).

Proverbs 2:4 says we should seek for the kingdom of God as silver and hidden treasure. In other words, we search for the wisdom of God as we would for something valuable and precious. When you realize you are truly dependent on God for all of your needs—food on your table, clothes on your back, the job you have, everything in your life—you go after Him and His ways with effort. You get passionate about your seeking. God becomes the primary thing in your life.

The more we seek Him, the more we love Him, and the more we love Him, the more we seek Him and the more we increase. It's a wonderful plan!

## Reflecting on His Goodness

A devoted seeker acts like the woman in Luke 15:8–9 who lost one of her ten silver coins. Why is the kingdom of God so precious?

_____

_____

_____

_____

_____

_____

_____

_____

_____

_____

_____

_____

_____

_____

_____

_____

_____

_____

_____

_____

*The kingdom of God is not a matter of eating and drinking, but of righteousness, peace and joy in the Holy Spirit, because anyone who serves Christ in this way is pleasing to God.*

(Romans 14:17–18 NIV)

## Experiencing His Goodness

Think of the one possession you have treasured most in your entire life. Now imagine what it would look like if you valued the things of God in the same way. Describe it here.

_____

_____

_____

_____

_____

_____

_____

_____

_____

_____

_____

_____

_____

_____

_____

_____

_____

_____

*When You said, "Seek My face," my heart said to You,*
*"Your face, LORD, I will seek."*
(Psalm 27:8 NKJV)

# Praying in His Goodness

*Day Four*

## God's Way of Getting Right

*For he [God] hath made him [Jesus] to be sin for us, who knew no sin;*
*that we might be made the righteousness of God in him.*
2 Corinthians 5:21

In the midst of my emphasis on obeying God, I want to make one thing perfectly clear. Christians do not earn right-standing with Him by doing good things. We receive that right-standing as a gift from God by believing and confessing that Jesus is our Lord.

When we put our faith in Jesus, something miraculous also happens in our hearts. We become new creations. What's more, because Jesus freed us from the power of sin, and because the Father has sent His own Holy Spirit to dwell within us, we actually have the ability to live godly lives.

First Covenant people were not changed on the inside. They could be counted righteous if they obeyed the Law, but even when they tried to obey, they couldn't do it for very long because their fallen nature would drag them back into disobedience. Throughout that era, because God loved people so, He longed for the day when that would change—the day when, through the blood of Jesus, His people would have a new heart so they could walk in His ways. Then He could bless them as richly as He desired. Thank God, we live in that day!

# Reflecting on His Goodness

The Greek for "born again" is literally "born from above." In what ways are the second birth superior to the first one, our natural birth?

_____

_____

_____

_____

_____

_____

_____

_____

_____

_____

_____

_____

_____

_____

_____

_____

_____

_____

_____

_____

_____

_____

*My little children, these things write I unto you, that ye sin not. And if any man sin,*
*we have an advocate with the Father, Jesus Christ the righteous.*

(1 John 2:1)

## Experiencing His Goodness

What "old ways" have you been delivered from
by the blood of Christ?

_____

_____

_____

_____

_____

_____

_____

_____

_____

_____

_____

_____

_____

_____

_____

*"This is the covenant I will make with the house of Israel after that time,"
declares the LORD. "I will put my law in their minds and write it on their hearts.
I will be their God, and they will be my people. No longer will a man teach his
neighbor, or a man his brother, saying, 'Know the LORD,' because they will all know
me, from the least of them to the greatest. . . . For I will forgive their wickedness and
will remember their sins no more."*

(Jeremiah 31:33–34 NIV)

# Praying in His Goodness

## Drawing Near

*Having therefore, brethren, boldness to enter into the holiest by the blood of Jesus,*
*by a new and living way, which he hath consecrated for us, through the vail,*
*that is to say, his flesh; and having an high priest over the house of God;*
*let us draw near with a true heart in full assurance of faith.*

Hebrews 10:19–22

As New Testament believers, we don't just read the Bible like a rule book and try to obey it. We know the Author! So we draw near to the One who wrote it and allow Him to speak to us. We seek Him until the words come alive in our hearts.

You see, God does not want you just to have a relationship with pen and ink. He wants you to have a relationship with Him!

For the Word of God to truly give us life, we must draw near to the person of God. We must trust that He will reward us with His manifest presence if we will earnestly seek Him.

One thing that will build your confidence is the realization that God has been seeking to have fellowship with mankind from the very beginning. When God provided the sacrifice of Jesus for us, He drew near to us in the most powerful way possible, and He made the way for us to draw near to Him. As we respond to God by seeking Him in return, we will discover we don't have to go very far to find Him. He's right here with us and in us.

## Reflecting on His Goodness

What error did the Pharisees make that we are all prone to make in our spiritual life? See John 5:39–40 for some insight.

_____

_____

_____

_____

_____

_____

_____

_____

_____

_____

_____

_____

_____

_____

_____

_____

_____

_____

_____

_____

_____

*But now in Christ Jesus ye who sometimes were far off are made nigh by the blood of Christ. For he is our peace.*

(Ephesians 2:13–14)

# Experiencing His Goodness

Are you sometimes reluctant to seek God? Why?

_____

_____

_____

_____

_____

_____

_____

_____

_____

_____

_____

_____

_____

_____

_____

_____

_____

_____

_____

_____

_____

_____

_____

_____

_____

*If I be lifted up from the earth, [I] will draw all men unto me.*

(John 12:32)

# Praying in His Goodness

## Looking for a Receiver

## Day One

❧

## How's Your Heart?

*For the eyes of the LORD run to and fro throughout the whole earth, to show himself strong in the behalf of them whose heart is perfect toward him.*

2 Chronicles 16:9

Again and again, the Scriptures teach us that God is unlimited in His resources and His abilities. He has placed enough riches in this earth to take care of everyone who will turn to Him. Our only concern is to develop our capacity to receive. We have to spiritually be in position by hearing and obeying God's Word.

God has in His hand blessings beyond human comprehension. He has spiritual victories He wants us to win. He has rewards and trophies He wants us to enjoy. But He cannot do it unless He can find someone to receive! God has to have a receiver!

Of course, I did not just learn that from a football game. I learned it from the Bible. Second Chronicles 16:9 says that God is constantly searching for that one whose heart is devoted to Him so that He might demonstrate His kindness and power in his or her life.

He will pick one person out of a million who will give his heart to Him, if that is all He can find—one person who, because of his heart condition, has the capacity to receive, and He will pour out His blessings upon him.

You can be that one!

# Reflecting on His Goodness

How did the woman with the issue of blood and Jairus, the synagogue ruler (both in Mark 5:22–34), position themselves to receive?

_____

_____

_____

_____

_____

_____

_____

_____

_____

_____

_____

_____

_____

_____

_____

_____

_____

_____

_____

_____

_____

_____

*If a man love me, he will keep my words: and my Father will love him, and we will come unto him, and make our abode with him.*

(John 14:23)

## Experiencing His Goodness

The word translated "perfect" in 2 Chronicles 16:9 means "devoted, faithful, dedicated, loyal, fully committed, consecrated." How does that affect your understanding of what God is looking for?

_____

_____

_____

_____

_____

_____

_____

_____

_____

_____

_____

_____

_____

_____

_____

_____

_____

_____

_____

_____

*Man looketh on the outward appearance, but the LORD looketh on the heart.*
(1 Samuel 16:7)

# Praying in His Goodness

*Day Two*

## One Mark of a Receiver

*Let God be true, but every man a liar.*
Romans 3:4

To be good receivers of God's Word, we must put forth the effort it takes to find out what God has said. As you discover what the Word says, permit it to enter your heart. Receive it like a gift from God. Let it change how you think and how you live. And remember this: every time you make a choice to receive and obey God's Word, you increase your spiritual capacity another notch.

Do not let natural, human reasoning or religious tradition cause you to resist the truth you see in God's Word. Determine beforehand that you are going to believe and welcome God's Word more than anybody else's opinions, word, or testimony. Decide in advance that if anybody's experience, including your own, seems to contradict the Word of God, you are going to throw out the experience and keep the Word.

If you will take that attitude and continue to welcome God's Word into your heart and meditate on it, you will grow strong in faith. You will become so assured that the Word is true, no one will be able to convince you otherwise.

## Reflecting on His Goodness

The parable of the sower (Mark 4:1–20) illustrates the difference between good receivers and bad receivers. Describe the four groups. What made the good receivers bear fruit?

_____

_____

_____

_____

_____

_____

_____

_____

_____

_____

_____

_____

_____

_____

_____

_____

_____

*My son, attend to my words; incline thine ear unto my sayings. Let them not depart from thine eyes; keep them in the midst of thine heart. For they are life unto those that find them, and health to all their flesh. Keep thy heart with all diligence; for out of it are the issues of life.*

(Proverbs 4:20–23)

## Experiencing His Goodness

According to Hebrews 4:12, why is the Word of God so essential?
Are you living as if your life depended on it?

_____

_____

_____

_____

_____

_____

_____

_____

_____

_____

_____

_____

_____

_____

_____

_____

_____

_____

*Brethren, whatever is true, whatever is worthy of reverence and is honorable and seemly, whatever is just, whatever is pure, whatever is lovely and lovable, whatever is kind and winsome and gracious, if there is any virtue and excellence, if there is anything worthy of praise, think on and weigh and take account of these things [fix your minds on them].*

(Philippians 4:8 AMP)

# Praying in His Goodness

## Day Three

## Perseverance Is Vital

*Faith is the assurance of things hoped for, the conviction of things not seen.*
Hebrews 11:1 NASB

If we're going to be good receivers, we cannot give up and stop believing God's Word when circumstances put us under pressure. When we get an evil report and we're told our illness has no cure, or we're about to go bankrupt, we have to be steadfast. We are believers! Believing God is what we do!

God has given us all the equipment necessary to believe. He has given us the fruit of the Spirit, which includes patience to help us stay strong until the answer comes. We have the wisdom of God available to us at all times just for the asking. We have Jesus Christ Himself at the right hand of the Father ever praying and interceding for us. We have a Father who loves us and is good all the time.

We have everything we need to walk by faith. It just takes some effort. We have to press in and refuse to quit. It takes time in some cases to see God's goodness become a reality in the midst of dark circumstances, but if we do not quit we will see God come shining through.

# Reflecting on His Goodness

Have you ever let difficulties deter you from having faith?
What did you learn about yourself in that experience? What did
you learn about God?

_____

_____

_____

_____

_____

_____

_____

_____

_____

_____

_____

_____

_____

_____

_____

_____

_____

_____

_____

_____

_____

*Hold fast what is good.*

(1 Thessalonians 5:21 NKJV)

# Experiencing His Goodness

How can you better put your spiritual "arsenal" to use
when hard times come?

_____
_____
_____
_____
_____
_____
_____
_____
_____
_____
_____
_____
_____
_____
_____
_____
_____
_____
_____
_____
_____
_____

*But the fruit of the [Holy] Spirit [the work which His presence within accomplishes]
is love, joy (gladness), peace, patience. . . .*
(Galatians 5:22 AMP)

# Praying in His Goodness

*Day Four*

## Making the Faith Connection

*Without faith it is impossible to please him: for he that cometh to God must believe that he is, and that he is a rewarder of them that diligently seek him.*

Hebrews 11:6

God isn't bothered by the boldness of the one who comes to Him in faith, because that boldness isn't inspired by the person's confidence in himself. It's inspired by his confidence in God—in His goodness, His love, and His power.

One of the best examples of such confidence can be found in Matthew 8:5–13, in the story of the Roman centurion. Not only did Jesus do what this man asked Him to do, He changed his plans in accordance with the man's next request. Jesus intended to go to his house and heal the servant, but the centurion said, in essence, "No, I'd rather You not come to my house because I'm not worthy. Just speak the Word and my servant will be healed."

The centurion put himself in position to receive. He heard and believed the Word about Jesus. He spoke words of faith, saying, "My servant will be healed." And he put action to his faith by coming to the Lord.

## Reflecting on His Goodness

Are you more like the people of Nazareth (Mark 6:1–6) or the people in Mark 5:22–34 and 10:46–52? Whose words, thoughts, and actions can you relate to when it comes to seeking the Lord?

_____
_____
_____
_____
_____
_____
_____
_____
_____
_____
_____
_____
_____
_____
_____
_____

*In [Christ Jesus our Lord] and through faith in him we may approach God with freedom and confidence.*

(Ephesians 3:12 NIV)

## Experiencing His Goodness

What do you need from God today? How can you put yourself in a
position to receive it?

_____

_____

_____

_____

_____

_____

_____

_____

_____

_____

_____

_____

_____

_____

_____

_____

_____

_____

_____

_____

_____

*Ask, and it will be given to you; seek, and you will find; knock,*
*and it will be opened to you.*

(Matthew 7:7 NKJV)

# Praying in His Goodness

## *Day Five*

## Don't Drop the Ball

*Be not afraid, only believe.*
Mark 5:36

I want to warn you of a particular thing that can hinder your ability to receive. You can be reaching out by faith for that Super Bowl pass of God's goodness. You can be well on your way to spiritual victory, but this devilish habit will cause you to drop the ball. Jesus warned us about it in Matthew 6:34: "Do not worry about tomorrow" (NIV).

One reason this instruction is so important is because you cannot worry and be in faith at the same time. Worry is a manifestation of fear, and fear contaminates your faith. It is, by definition, doubting that God is going to come through for you. Obviously, faith and doubt cannot dwell together in the same heart. One of them will have to go. Your heart is your responsibility—you choose.

When thoughts of worry or fear come, don't give them any place. Reject them. Get your Bible and look up the Scriptures you are believing. Carry them with you so when you're bombarded with doubt or bad news, you have the Word right there to help you.

# Reflecting on His Goodness

Peter's experience with faith and fear in Matthew 14:25–32 represents our universal struggle. What lessons do you glean as you reread this account?

_____

_____

_____

_____

_____

_____

_____

_____

_____

_____

_____

_____

_____

_____

_____

_____

_____

_____

_____

*Be anxious for nothing, but in everything by prayer and supplication, with thanksgiving, let your requests be made known to God.*

(Philippians 4:6 NKJV)

## Experiencing His Goodness

Andrew Murray wrote years ago, "I am going to do the will of God every day without thinking of tomorrow." What situation are you facing today that needs this wisdom?

_____

_____

_____

_____

_____

_____

_____

_____

_____

_____

_____

_____

_____

_____

_____

_____

_____

_____

_____

_____

_____

_____

*Cast all your anxiety on him because he cares for you.*

(1 Peter 5:7 NIV)

# Praying in His Goodness

## The New Song

### Day One

## Opening the Door

*O sing unto the LORD a new song: sing unto the LORD, all the earth. Sing unto the
LORD, bless his name; show forth his salvation from day to day.*
Psalm 96:1–2

I want to give you a spiritual key that will help you receive as much of
God's goodness as you can as quickly as possible. Practice it and it will accel-
erate your spiritual development. It will increase your capacity to receive from
God. It will open the way for His blessing to flood your life more fully and
more quickly.

What is this wonderful thing that will so enhance your life? Singing a new
song.

Even if you were just born again five minutes ago, you have reason to
rejoice. After all, you are not on the road to hell anymore. You are on the road
to heaven! You have a covenant with Almighty God and He has promised to
bless you, heal you, prosper you, and deliver you! Where you once were hope-
less, now you have a sure hope in Him!

Problems or not, you are in a great place! So speed up the process by singing to the One who delivers you from all your fears and evil circumstances.

# Reflecting on His Goodness

Everyone's "song" comes in a different form, depending on each person's gifts and experiences. Think of some of the people you know and how they express their praise, and then name as many forms of praise as you can think of.

_____

_____

_____

_____

_____

_____

_____

_____

_____

_____

_____

_____

_____

_____

_____

_____

_____

_____

_____

*Sing joyfully to the LORD, you righteous; it is fitting for the upright to praise him....*
*For the word of the LORD is right and true; he is faithful in all he does. The LORD*
*loves righteousness and justice; the earth is full of his unfailing love.*

(Psalm 33:1, 4–5 NIV)

## Experiencing His Goodness

What are your reasons for praise? Build a list and keep adding to it so that you have something to refer to whenever you're discouraged.

_____

_____

_____

_____

_____

_____

_____

_____

_____

_____

_____

_____

_____

_____

_____

_____

_____

_____

_____

_____

_____

*Whoever is wise will observe these things, and they will understand the lovingkindness of the LORD.*

(Psalm 107:43 NKJV)

# Praying in His Goodness

# Day Two

## Sharing the Song

*I waited patiently for the LORD; and he inclined unto me, and heard my cry. . . .*
*He hath put a new song in my mouth, even praise unto our God: many shall see it,*
*and fear, and shall trust in the LORD.*

Psalm 40:1, 3

God Himself has put a new song in your mouth. If you will just open your mouth by faith and start singing God's praises, you'll find words coming up out of your heart. Just sing the truth about God. Sing about how wonderful and good He is. Sing His Word back to Him. The more you sing, the more His words will flow, and you will realize you had a new song inside all along. Your song will build you up and strengthen you.

I personally don't sing to people; I sing to the Lord. When I'm around others, I speak my new song. I say words of thanksgiving and praise about Him.

You ought to do the same thing. Whether you choose to sing or just to speak your new song, everybody around you ought to hear it. If you are born again, you should always have a song of salvation, a song of thanksgiving, a song of deliverance, a song of healing, and a song of prosperity.

The new song comes out of your heart.

## Reflecting on His Goodness

When the people of God start singing and speaking His praises, many people hear and put their trust in Him. Why do our personal stories often reach people better than our "preaching"?

_____

_____

_____

_____

_____

_____

_____

_____

_____

_____

_____

_____

_____

_____

_____

_____

_____

*Declare his glory among the heathen, his wonders among all people. For the LORD is great, and greatly to be praised.*

(Psalm 96:3–4)

## Experiencing His Goodness

Write a statement that could serve as your opening line to each of the types of songs mentioned in the devotional: *a song of salvation, a song of thanksgiving, a song of deliverance, a song of healing, and a song of prosperity.*

*I will praise You, for I am fearfully and wonderfully made; marvelous are Your works, and that my soul knows very well.*

(Psalm 139:14 NKJV)

# Praying in His Goodness

*Day Three*

## Making God Big

*Then [Ezra] told them, Go your way, eat the fat, drink the sweet drink, and send
portions to him for whom nothing is prepared: for this day is holy to our Lord. And be
not grieved and depressed, for the joy of the Lord is your strength and stronghold.*
Nehemiah 8:10 AMP

Some people miss the blessing the new song brings because they keep
singing the same old song: "Poor me. Nothing good ever happens to me. I'm
broke. I'm sick. I don't know why God doesn't take care of me."

Don't sing that kind of song anymore. It's out of date. Instead, voice praise
and thanksgiving. After all, God is never the problem. He is always good. He
is always on time. He never misses it. So we ought to be magnifying Him all
the time.

To magnify the Lord means to focus your heart, mind, and mouth on Him
until He is the biggest thing in your life. It means to make Him big in your own
sight. You can do that by talking about how great and good He is.

The fact is, no matter how much you magnify God, you will never be
able to make Him as big as He really is. God is so big, we will spend eternity
exploring Him. He's so great, He exceeds our greatest expectations. He's so
good that no matter how good we think He is, we will continually discover
He's better than we thought!

## Reflecting on His Goodness

Read Numbers 12, 1 Corinthians 10:9–10, and James 5:9. How seriously does grumbling offend God? What have been some of the consequences of people's grumbling and complaining?

_And out of them shall proceed thanksgiving and the voice of them that make merry: and I will multiply them, and they shall not be few; I will also glorify them, and they shall not be small._

(Jeremiah 30:19)

## Experiencing His Goodness

One way to magnify the Lord is to simply speak the truth about Him. What are some biblical truths you can claim before God and others?

_____

_____

_____

_____

_____

_____

_____

_____

_____

_____

_____

_____

_____

_____

_____

_____

_____

_____

_____

_____

_____

_____

*Let them shout for joy, and be glad, that favour my righteous cause: yea,*
*let them say continually, Let the LORD be magnified.*

(Psalm 35:27)

# Praying in His Goodness

# Day Four

## When Life Is Like a Dream

*When the Lord turned again the captivity of Zion, we were like them that dream. Then was our mouth filled with laughter, and our tongue with singing: then said they among the heathen, The LORD hath done great things for them.*

Psalm 126:1–2

As believers we should be continually thanking God for what He's done for us. We should be singing in the shower, singing in our cars, singing as we go about our work.

That's the way God wants us to be. He wants us so full of His praises that no one has to lead us, no one has to urge us, but we sing to Him because we can't help ourselves.

If you will do it wholeheartedly, before long, you will start remembering how bad things were when you found God. You will start thinking about what He has done for you since then. You will get excited about what He is going to do for you in the days ahead and you will want to sing!

If you will keep singing that song, you will find yourself walking in your dreams. You will look around and see the goodness of God poured out in every area of your life. You will be living out His plan, enjoying His provision, and dwelling in the place He prepared especially for you.

You will be living proof to the world that "happy is that people...whose God is the LORD" (Psalm 144:15).

## Reflecting on His Goodness

Why is it important to praise the Lord even when we don't feel like it?
What usually happens when we ignore our feelings and
do as God asks?

_____

_____

_____

_____

_____

_____

_____

_____

_____

_____

_____

_____

_____

_____

_____

_____

_____

_____

_____

_____

_____

*Rejoice in the Lord always. Again I will say, rejoice!*

(Philippians 4:4 NKJV)

## Experiencing His Goodness

Compare your past and present and then express how far God has
brought you by either creating your own song lyrics or writing down
the lyrics of a favorite song that describes your journey.
Then sing it to the Lord.

_____

_____

_____

_____

_____

_____

_____

_____

_____

_____

_____

_____

_____

_____

_____

_____

*Enter into his gates with thanksgiving, and into his courts with praise: be thankful
unto him, and bless his name. For the LORD is good; his mercy is everlasting;
and his truth endureth to all generations.*

(Psalm 100:4–5)

## Praying in His Goodness

## Day Five

## God's Goodness Includes You

*Ye that fear the LORD, trust in the LORD: he is their help and their shield. . . .*
*He will bless them that fear the LORD, both small and great. The LORD shall*
*increase you more and more, you and your children. Ye are blessed of the LORD*
*which made heaven and earth. The heaven, even the heavens, are the LORD's:*
*but the earth hath he given to the children of men.*

Psalm 115:11, 13–16

God has you on His mind. He is thinking about your increase and the good He would enjoy bringing into your life. Stretch out your hands toward heaven, the place from which comes your help. Put yourself in position to receive all that God desires to do in your life. You will be able to say with David, the man after God's own heart: "I will extol thee, my God, O king; and I will bless thy name for ever and ever. Every day will I bless thee; and I will praise thy name for ever and ever. Great is the LORD, and greatly to be praised; and his greatness is unsearchable. . . . The LORD is good to all: and his tender mercies are over all his works" (Psalm 145:1–3, 9).

God is good to all. That means you!

## Reflecting on His Goodness

How has your belief in God's goodness changed over the course of this devotional experience? Do you now understand that His goodness extends to you?

_____

_____

_____

_____

_____

_____

_____

_____

_____

_____

_____

_____

_____

_____

_____

_____

_____

_____

*The LORD is nigh unto all them that call upon him, to all that call upon him in truth. He will fulfill the desire of them that fear him: he also will hear their cry, and will save them. The LORD preserveth all them that love him.*

(Psalm 145:18–20)

## Experiencing His Goodness

How has your experience of God's goodness increased as you've worked through this journal? How can you keep moving forward in your journey with the Lord?

_____

_____

_____

_____

_____

_____

_____

_____

_____

_____

_____

_____

_____

_____

_____

_____

_____

*As ye have therefore received Christ Jesus the Lord, so walk ye in him: rooted and built up in him, and stablished in the faith, as ye have been taught, abounding therein with thanksgiving.*

(Colossians 2:6–7)

# Praying in His Goodness